MY BIG, CRAZY DRAWING & DOODLE BOOK

An interactive adventure with more than 100 creative ideas for tons of doodling fun

www.walterfoster.com
Walter Foster Jr.,
an imprint of Quarto Publishing Group USA Inc.
6 Orchard Road, Suite 100
Lake Forest, CA 92630

Artwork © 2015 Green Android, Ltd.
Illustrated by Fiona Gowen
Photographs © Shutterstock

Publisher: Rebecca J. Razo
Creative Director: Shelley Baugh
Production Director: Yuhong Guo
Senior Editor: Stephanie Meissner
Managing Editor: Karen Julian
Editorial Director: Pauline Molinari
Associate Editor: Jennifer Gaudet
Developmental Editor: Janessa Osle
Editorial Assistant: Julie Chapa
Production Manager: Nicole Szawlowski
Production Designer: Debbie Aiken

Printed in Shenzhen, China
1 3 5 7 9 10 8 6 4 2
19258

TABLE OF CONTENTS

Welcome to Your Big, Crazy Drawing & Doodle Book!......... 4

Basic Tools & Materials 6

How to Use This Book 7

Warm-Up Exercises 8

Faces & Places 11

Crazy Portraits..55

Funny Foods 67

Sweet Treats 105

The End 128

WELCOME TO YOUR BIG, CRAZY DRAWING & DOODLE BOOK!

This doodle journal is your personal space to expand your imagination and express your creativity—in a big, crazy style that's uniquely yours! In the pages of **My Big, Crazy Drawing & Doodle Book** you'll find photographs, illustrations, and open practice pages featuring everyday objects in need of a little imagination. You'll be invited to reinterpret and accessorize common subjects in your everyday life and, along the way, learn that creativity is waiting to be found anywhere in our big, crazy world. All you need to do is grab your art tools and start exploring!

BASIC TOOLS & MATERIALS

You can start every doodle with a drawing pencil. Then use markers, colored pencils, or even paint to add color!

drawing pencil and paper

eraser

sharpener

colored pencils

felt-tip markers

paintbrushes and paints

HOW TO USE THIS BOOK

Each section of this book is devoted to different common subjects in daily life. Practice your doodles directly on the page using the templates and open spaces provided. The prompts will give you a place to start and are there simply to inspire your creativity—it's up to you whether you want to use crayons, markers, colored pencils, or paints to bring them to life!

WARM-UP EXERCISES

Most doodles are made up of basic shapes, such as circles, triangles, and rectangles. Nearly everything you draw can begin with a simple shape!

CIRCLES are perfect for clocks and fruit

RECTANGLES are good for robots and gadgets

OTHER SIMPLE SHAPES

Clouds are easy to draw, and they make good backgrounds. No two clouds need to look exactly alike!

GROW A DOODLE

Continuing simple doodles by "growing" them across your page creates unique patterns to add to your drawings. Add leaves and flowers for extra detail.

Before you begin, warm up your hand by drawing squiggles and shapes.

FACES + PLACES

People are everywhere, and this makes them one of the best sources for inspiration! There are endless ways you can transform a little doodle by simply giving it a funny hairdo, a unique expression, or some quirky features. Places are great too; they allow your doodles to travel anywhere you like! This section will help you give personality to your drawings. You'll find everything from moustaches to hats to googly eyes, along with a variety of backgrounds and scenes, all ready for you to leave your creative mark.

DRAW THE FEATURES ON THESE FACES TO MATCH THE EXPRESSIONS LISTED BELOW.

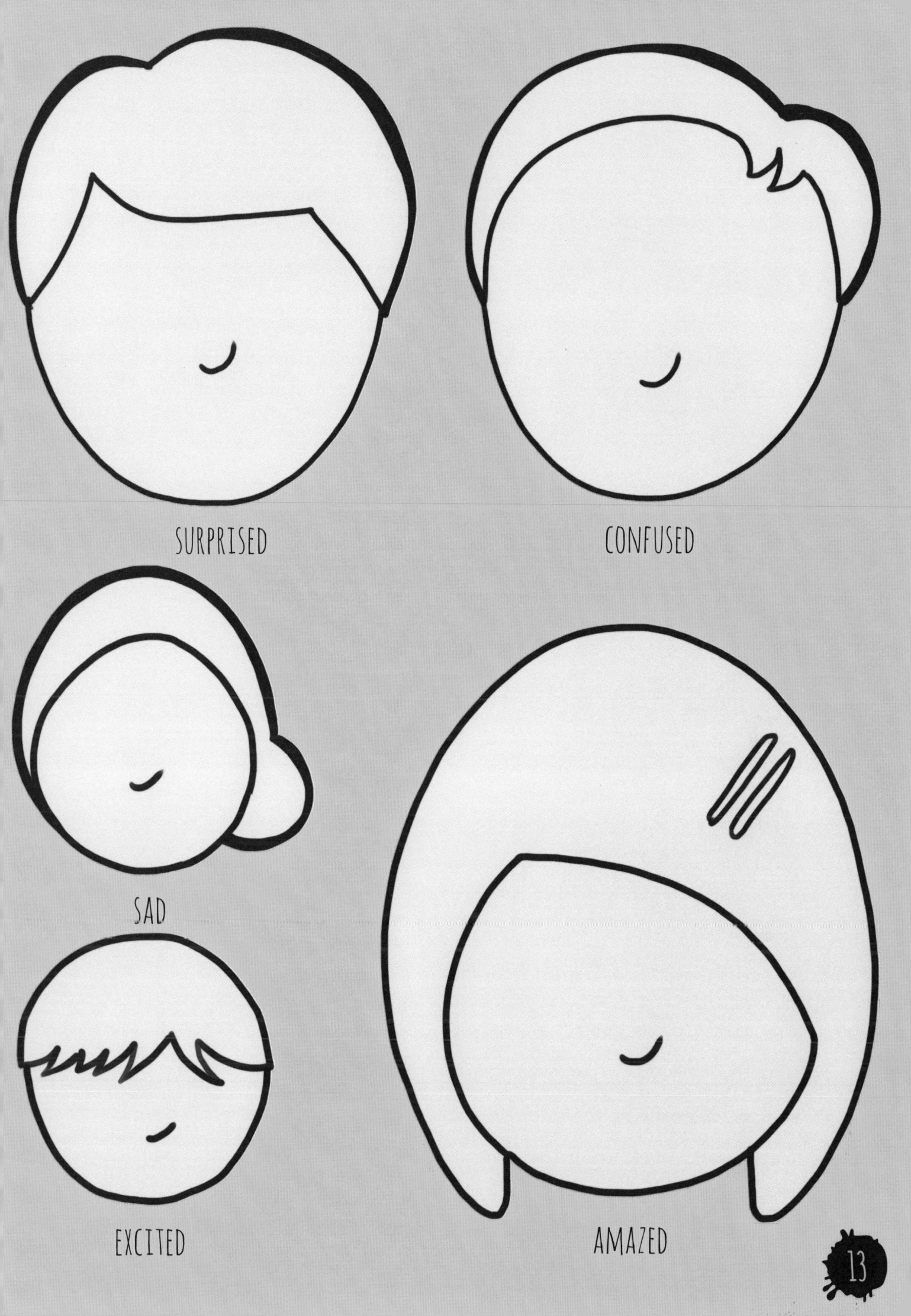

NOW MAKE UP YOUR OWN EXPRESSIONS TO WRITE ON THE BLANK LINES BELOW, AND THEN DOODLE THEM IN!

_____   _____

_____   _____

ADD SOME CRAZY HAIRDOS TO THE FACES BELOW!

Color in the PASSPORT pictures.

ADD SOME **FUNNY FACES** TO THESE HANDS AND FINGERS.

IMAGINE YOU'RE IN DISGUISE. THEN DRAW WHAT YOUR FACE WOULD LOOK LIKE IN EACH PAIR OF CRAZY GLASSES.

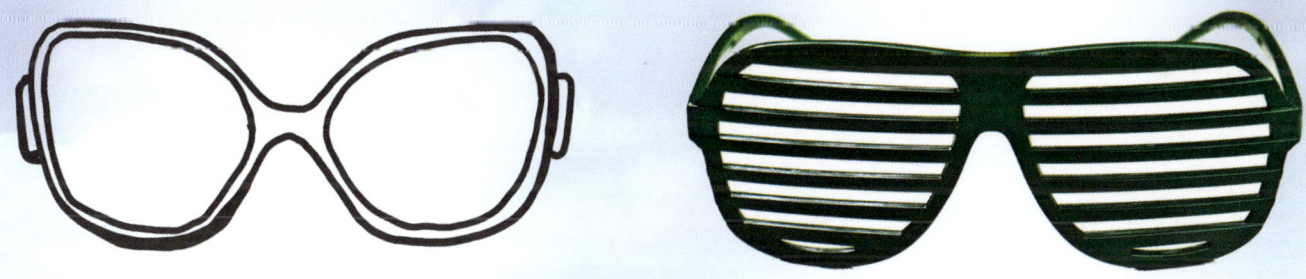

We "MOUSTACHE" YOU A QUESTION. HOW MANY DIFFERENT TYPES OF **BEARDS** AND **MOUSTACHES** CAN YOU CREATE FOR THESE FACES?

MAKE THEM AS WACKY AS YOU WANT!

THESE HATS NEED HEADS AND FACES. DRAW THEM IN THE SPACES BELOW!

ADD SOME GOOGLY EYES TO THESE FACES.

HOW ABOUT SOME BIG, TOOTHY GRINS FOR THE FACES BELOW!?

Add doodly ARMS, LEGS, and FACES to these shapes. Give each one its own expression and personality!

CAN YOU TURN THESE SCRIBBLES INTO PEOPLE? GIVE IT A TRY!

NOW **DOODLE** YOUR OWN SCRIBBLES WITH COLORED PENCILS, MARKERS, OR CRAYONS; THEN DESIGN THEIR PERSONALITIES.

Turn these **THUMBPRINTS** and **PAINT SPLOTCHES** into little people and animals. Maybe some of them can become cartoon characters or even **SUPERHEROES!**

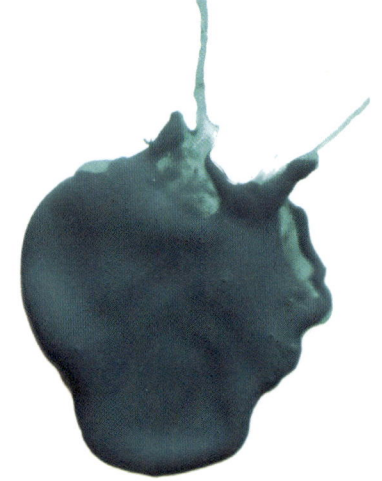

USE YOUR IMAGINATION TO DOODLE AROUND THE **BUILDINGS** SHOWN BELOW. ADD **BACKGROUNDS, CARS,** AND **PEOPLE**—BE CREATIVE AND HAVE FUN!

In the country...

In the suburbs...

In the city...

These **BUILDINGS** are all famous **LANDMARKS** from different **WORLD CITIES**. Doodle yourself and some friends exploring and taking in the sights!

47

DRAW YOURSELF EXPLORING THESE FAMOUS BUILDINGS. WHAT OTHER FAMOUS LANDMARKS CAN YOU THINK OF? DOODLE THEM ON THE NEXT PAGE!

Draw the BONES on these X-RAYS.

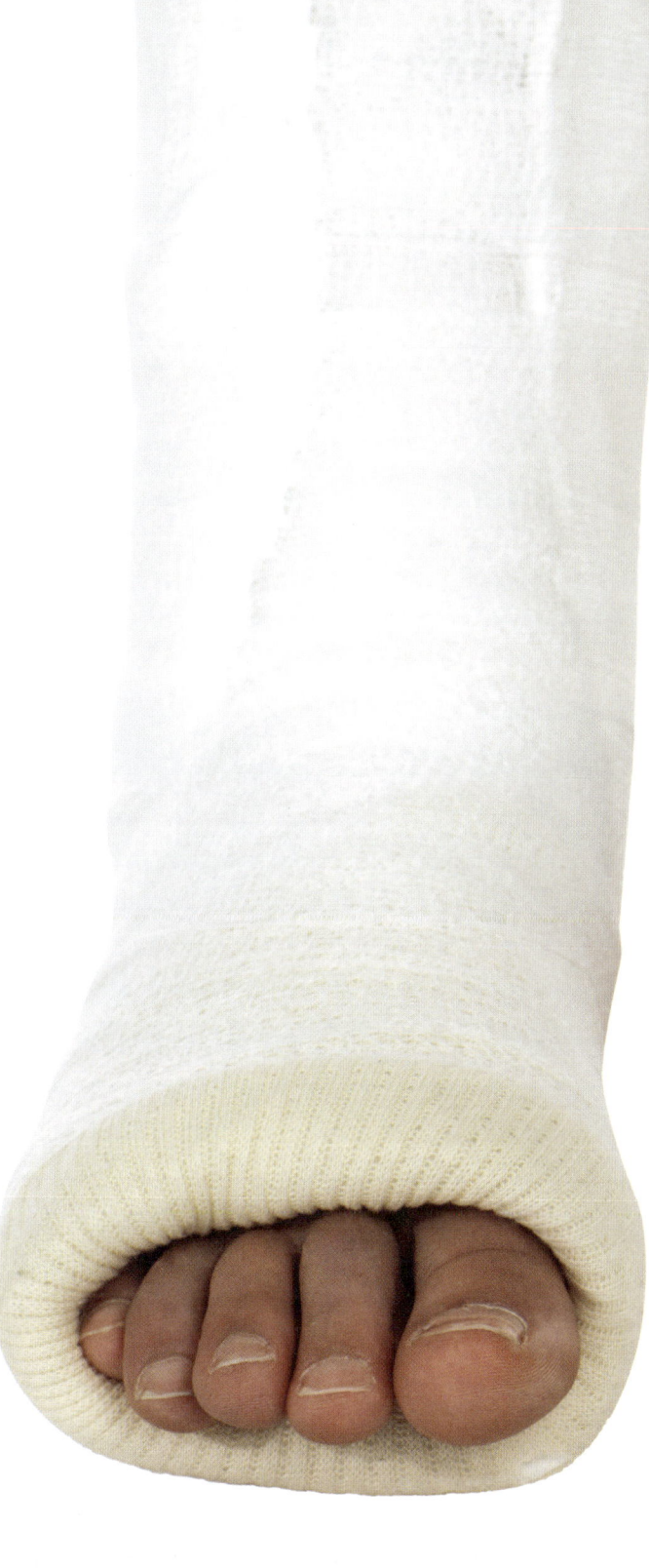

Your FRIEND has broken his leg. Draw a HAPPY PICTURE on the cast to make him feel better!

IMAGINE YOU'RE A FASHION DESIGNER CREATING TRENDY T-SHIRTS. DOODLE YOUR IDEAS BELOW.

CRAZY PORTRAITS

Now that you've practiced bringing personality to your doodles, you're ready to zoom in and take an even closer look. This section has prompts that focus on individual portraits of people you know very, very well—and others you imagine you do. You'll reimagine drawings of family members, your favorite characters, and many more. This is a great time to try out different art mediums like markers or paint if you haven't already—start your portraits by outlining in pencil, and then bring them to life on the page with color!

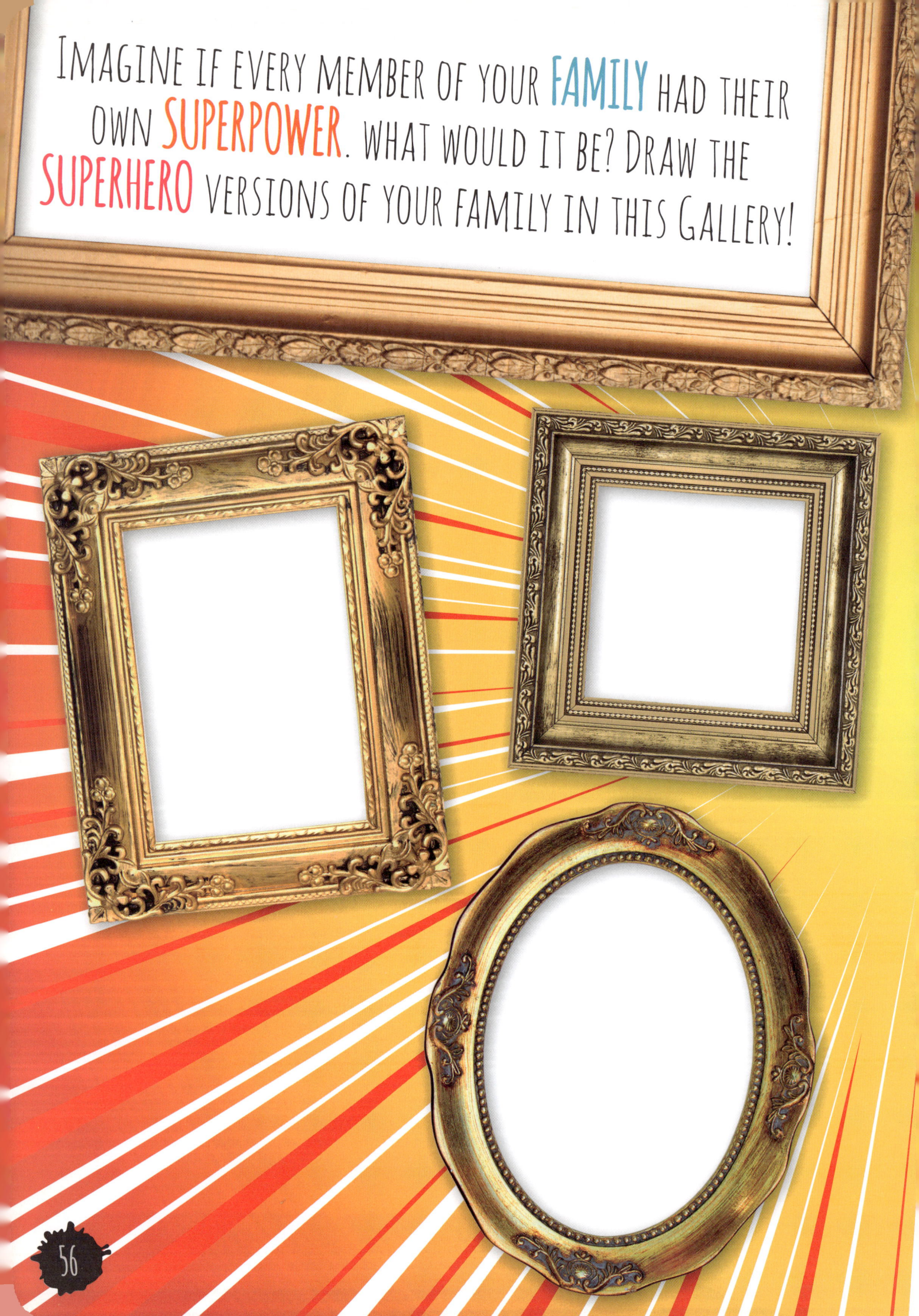

DESIGN YOUR OWN STAMPS BELOW!

Wanted

Draw the meanest, baddest OUTLAW you can think of for this WANTED POSTER.

Reward

$5000

Celebrity Scrapbook

Doodle your favorite **celebrities** or **characters** from movies, TV shows, and books.

WHAT WILL YOU LOOK LIKE WHEN YOU'RE OLDER?

DRAW A PORTRAIT OF YOURSELF AS A GROWN-UP.

Funny Foods

Sometimes the brightest, most eye-catching colors and designs are right in front of you: in the kitchen...at mealtime...even on your plate! This section makes food fun—you'll work up a creative appetite (and maybe a real one too) and learn to bring a humorous, whimsical touch to everything you eat and drink. Whether you design your own soda brand or draw a secret message in your alphabet soup, imagination can make even your vegetables funny and charming!

COLOR IN THESE ROWS OF TASTY **FRUITS** IN COORDINATING SHADES TO MAKE A COOL **PATTERN**!

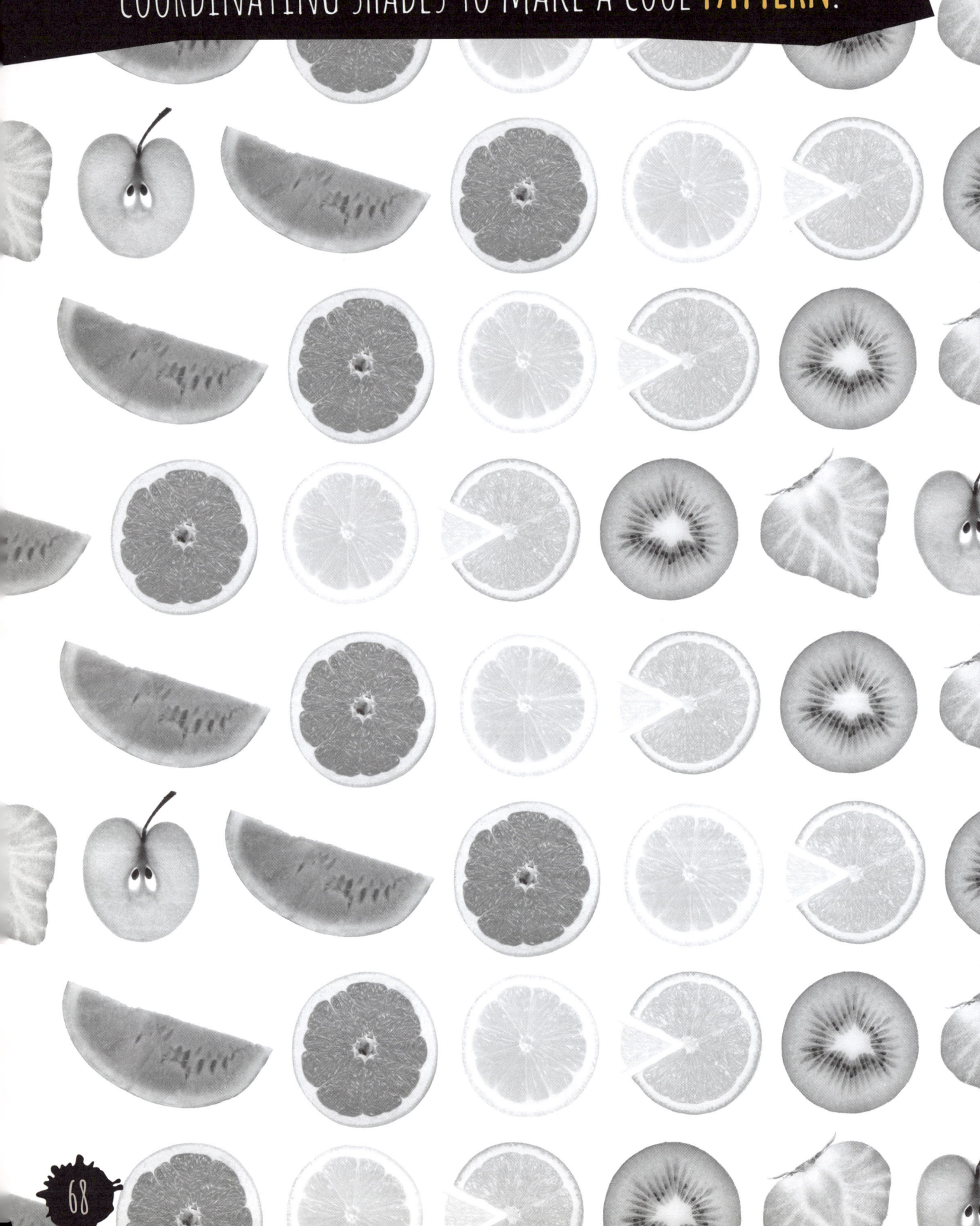

Can you add some COLOR to the FOOD in these jars? Then CREATE your own in the empty JARS below!

WHAT WOULD YOU HATE TO EAT?

DRAW THE MOST DISGUSTING DINNER YOU CAN IMAGINE.

DON'T FORGET TO COLOR IN THE BOWL!

If you invented a new DRESSING, FLAVOR, or SAUCE, what would it be? Draw your ideas on the blank PACKETS and BOTTLES below!

WHAT GOES IN THE **KITCHEN DRAWERS**?

DOODLE THE OBJECTS YOU EXPECT TO SEE.

WHAT **SHOULDN'T** BE IN **KITCHEN DRAWERS**? THINK OF THINGS THAT DON'T BELONG AND **DOODLE** THEM!

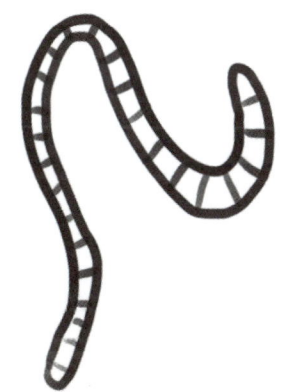

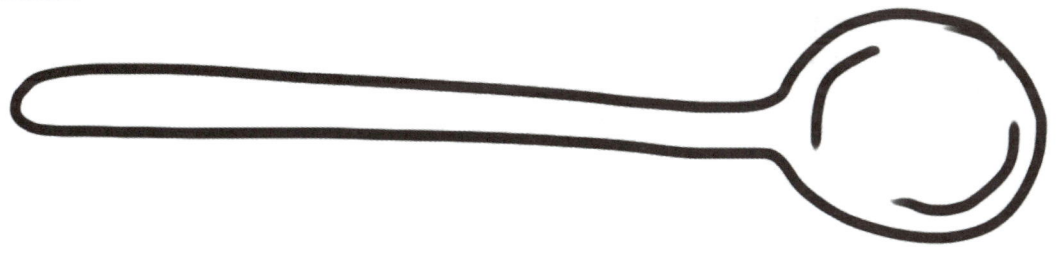

WHAT'S COOKING? DRAW IT INSIDE THIS OVEN.

WHAT'S IN YOUR FRIDGE?
DRAW IT ON THESE PAGES.

IF YOU HAD YOUR VERY OWN **SODA COMPANY**, WHAT WOULD IT BE CALLED? WHAT KIND OF FUN, **FIZZY DRINK** WOULD YOU MAKE? PRACTICE BELOW AND **DOODLE** YOUR ORIGINAL **NAME**, **LOGO**, AND **LABELS** ON THE EMPTY CANS ON THE NEXT PAGE.

FILL the **BLENDER!** Draw the **INGREDIENTS**— fruits, veggies, anything you like— in the space below; then **COLOR** in the blender with whatever you think your ingredients would look like all **MIXED TOGETHER!**

CREATE THE WORLD'S WACKIEST PIZZA!

COVER THIS REFRIGERATOR DOOR WITH MAGNETS AND FUNNY DOODLES.

WHAT'S FOR DINNER? FILL THESE POTS WITH SCRUMPTIOUS FOOD.

IF YOU COULD EAT ALL OF YOUR FAVORITE **FOODS** AND **SNACKS** AT THE SAME TIME, WHAT WOULD YOU HAVE?

FILL THESE **PLATES** WITH YOUR OWN FANTASY **FEAST**.

ADD SOME VEGETABLES TO CHOP ON THE CUTTING BOARD BELOW.

NOW IT'S TIME TO MAKE YOUR SALAD! DOODLE A SUPER SILLY SALAD COMPLETE WITH PROPS AND EXPRESSIONS ON THE VEGGIES BELOW!

SWEET TREATS

The best kind of ending is always dessert, right? This last section gives you plenty of sweet treats to decorate and embellish with your doodles—including cupcakes, gingerbread men (and ladies), doughnuts, and more. To add extra impact to your drawings, try coloring in the dessert with colored pencils and adding the toppings or icing with markers! Your sweet treats can be realistic and resemble baked goods you would actually want to eat, or they can be as silly and wild looking as you like. The only goal is to transform everyday life with creativity and imagination!

FILL THE **CONES** WITH YUMMY **ICE CREAM**. DON'T FORGET TASTY TOPPINGS!

IMAGINE YOU'RE HAVING A **BAKE SALE!** DECORATE THESE **CUPCAKES** BY ADDING ICING, SPRINKLES, AND CANDIES.

THE HOLIDAYS ARE FULL OF SWEET TREATS TO DECORATE. CAN YOU ADD SOME FUN, FESTIVE DESIGNS TO THE COOKIES BELOW?

IMAGINE THIS FRESH BATCH OF **COOKIES** IS FILLED WITH DAPPER **GINGERBREAD** MEN AND CHARMING LADIES. ADD **ACCESSORIES**, SUCH AS MOUSTACHES, TOP HATS, BOW TIES, AND PRETTY DRESSES—THEN SET THEM ALL LOOSE FOR A NIGHT OUT ON THE TOWN!

IT'S TIME FOR A MILKSHAKE! DOODLE THE MOST DELICIOUS ONE YOU CAN THINK OF.

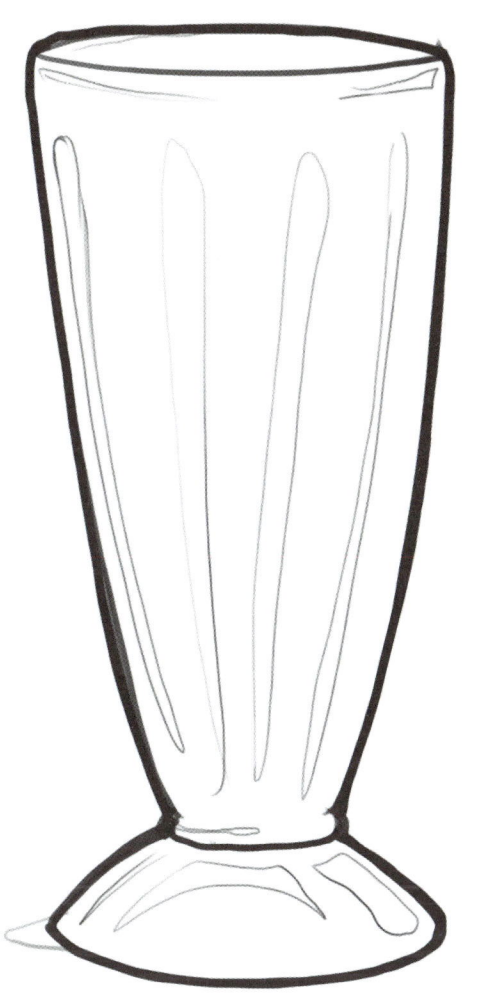
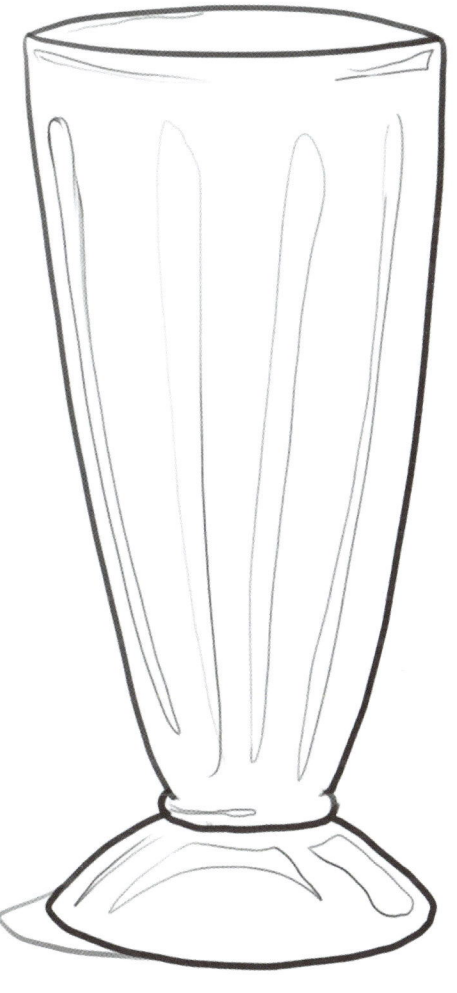
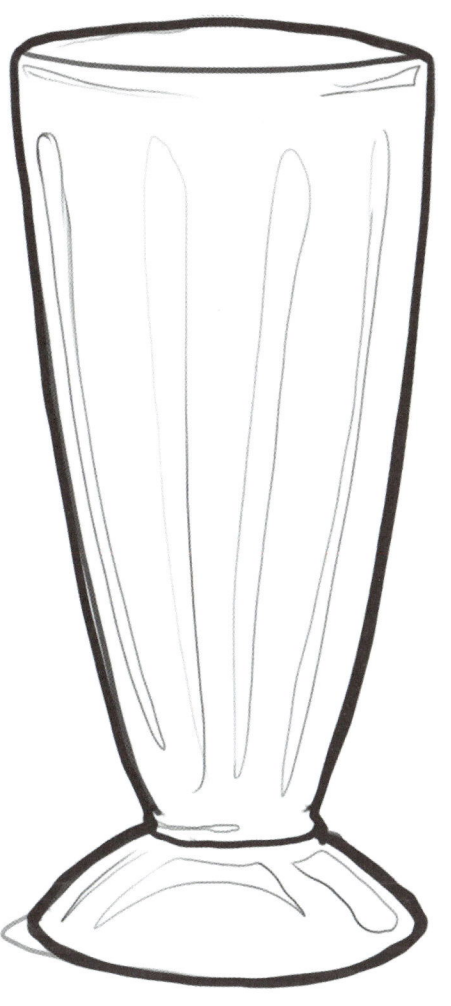

DON'T FORGET TO ADD **WHIPPED CREAM** AND **SPRINKLES**!

DESIGN A FABULOUS **BIRTHDAY** CAKE FOR YOUR BEST FRIEND!

ON THE BLANK LINES BELOW, MAKE UP YOUR OWN **FLAVORS** FOR THESE MACAROONS. THEN PRACTICE **DOODLING** YOUR OWN MACAROONS ON THE OPPOSITE PAGE!

IMAGINE YOU'RE MAKING YOUR OWN CANDY. DRAW IN CRAZY STRIPES AND SWIRLS ON THE WRAPPERS, AND THEN ADD BRIGHT COLORS!

DESIGN YOUR OWN CHOCOLATE BAR LABEL! PRACTICE DOODLING THE NAME OF YOUR BRAND AND LOGO IN THE SPACE BELOW; THEN TRANSFER IT TO THE WRAPPER ON THE NEXT PAGE.

THE END

You've designed, drawn, and doodled everything from your own T-shirt to a superhero family portrait and a super silly salad. Hopefully along the way you have learned that creativity and imagination can transform everyday life! This is only the beginning of your artistic adventures in the big, crazy world of creativity. Continue exploring and developing your own style by drawing inspiration from the people you meet, the places you go, and the objects around you—there's no limit to what you can create!